the WONDROUS

RESTORATION

Darryl Quinn

"IF ANY OF YOU LACK WISDOM...

... LET HIM ASK OF GOD"

JS-H 1:11

"JOSEPH... THIS IS
MY BELOVED SON...
HEAR HIM"

JS-H 1:17

"JOSEPH..."

JS-H 1:30

THE ANGEL MORONI VISITED JOSEPH. HE HAD AN IMPORTANT MESSAGE FROM GOD.

JS-H 1:33

JS-H 1:48

JS-H 1:49-50

THE SMITH FAMILY
SERVED THE LORD
AND LISTENED TO
HIS WORDS.

JS-H 1:50

JS-H 1:51-54

JS-H 1:57

THE TIME WAS RIGHT TO BEGIN GOD'S WORK

JS-H 1:59

JS-H 1:67

HEAVENLY MESSENGERS RESTORED PRIESTHOOD KEYS

JS-H 1:68-69

JS-H 1:68-69

JS-H 1:70-71

D&C 19:26

JOSEPH HAD FAITH EVEN WHEN OTHERS DIDN'T

D&C 105:38-41

D&C 109:8

THE LORD WAS WITH JOSEPH
D&C 110:2-4

. . . ALWAYS

D&C 122:9

THE LORD PREPARED THE SAINTS FOR A NEW HOME

D&C 136:1-10

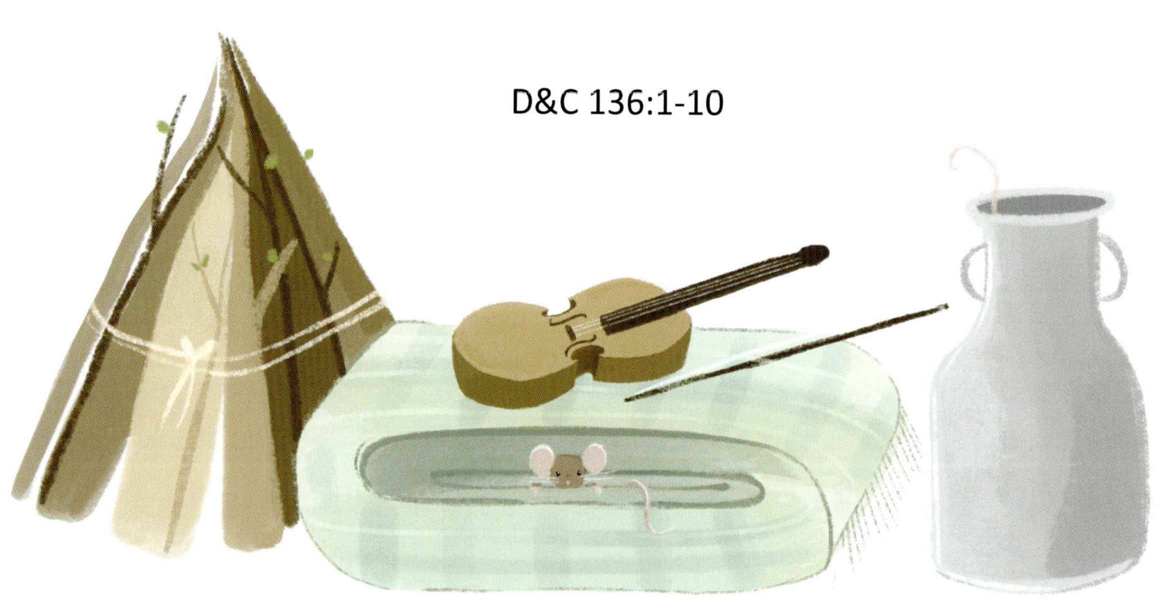

D&C 136:11

Isaiah 2:2

Isaiah 2:3

FAMILIES ARE FOREVER

Matthew 16:19

For my children

ISBN 13: 978-1-4621-3960-6

Published by CFI, an imprint of Cedar Fort, Inc.
2373 W. 700 S., Springville, UT 84663
Distributed by Cedar Fort, Inc., www.cedarfort.com

Printed in the United States of America

10 9 8 7 6 5 4 3 2 1

Printed on acid-free paper